learn to draw
Pets

Step-by-step instructions for
more than 25 cute and cuddly animals

ILLUSTRATED BY ROBBIN CUDDY

This library edition published in 2015 by Walter Foster Jr.,
an imprint of Quarto Publishing Group USA Inc.
3 Wrigley, Suite A
Irvine, CA 92618

Distributed in the United States and Canada by
Lerner Publisher Services
241 First Avenue North
Minneapolis, MN 55401 U.S.A.
www.lernerbooks.com

First Library Edition

Library of Congress Cataloging-in-Publication Data

Learn to draw pets : step-by-step instructions for more than 25 cute and cuddly animals /
illustrated by Robbin Cuddy. -- 1st library ed.
     pages cm
  ISBN 978-1-939581-53-2
1. Animals in art--Juvenile literature. 2. Drawing--Technique--Juvenile literature. I. Cuddy,
Robbin, illustrator.
  NC783.8.P48L43 2015
  743.6--dc23

                                                                          2014028486

062015
18882

9 8 7 6 5 4 3 2 1

Table of Contents

Tools & Materials

There's more than one way to bring favorite pets to life on paper—
you can use crayons, markers, colored pencils, or even paints.
Just be sure you have plenty of good "animal colors"—
black, blue, brown, gray, orange, purple, white, and yellow.

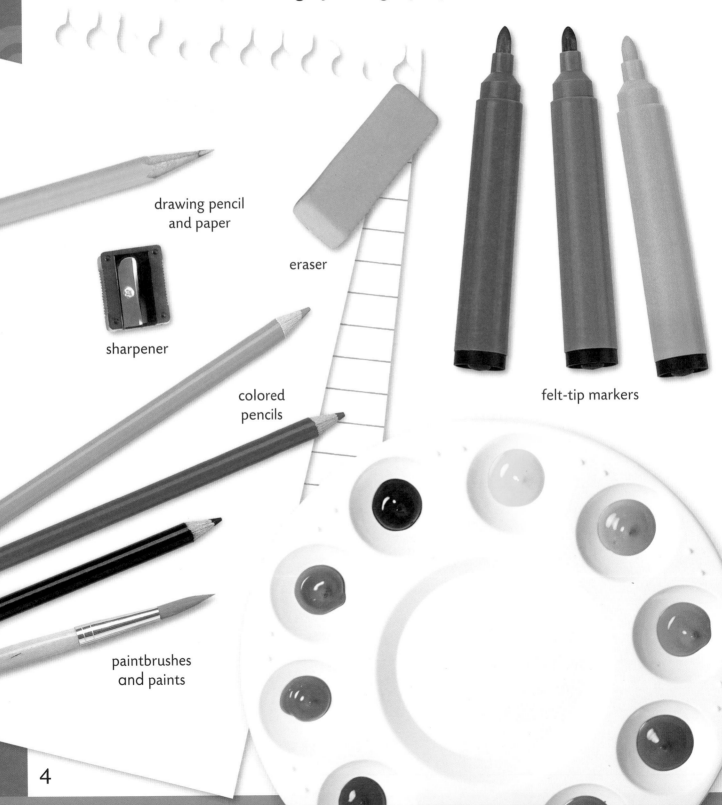

drawing pencil
and paper

eraser

sharpener

colored
pencils

felt-tip markers

paintbrushes
and paints

How to Use This Book

The drawings in this book are made up of basic shapes, such as circles, triangles, and rectangles. Practice drawing the shapes below.

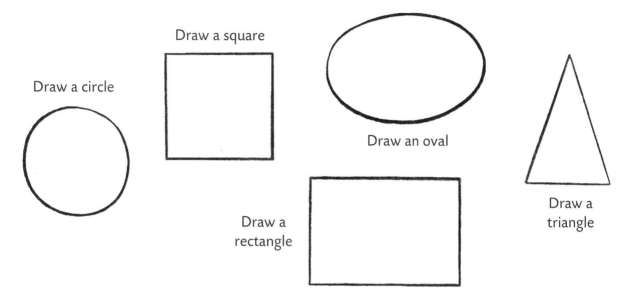

Draw a square

Draw a circle

Draw an oval

Draw a rectangle

Draw a triangle

Notice how these drawings begin with basic shapes.

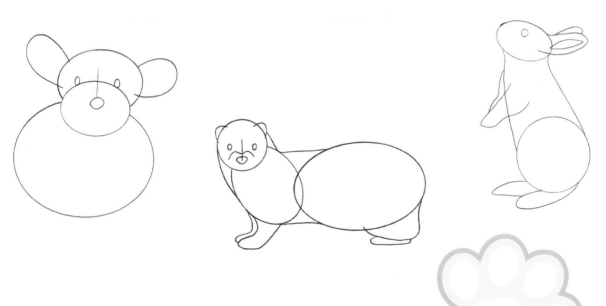

In this book, you'll learn about the size, location, diet, and appearance of each featured animal. Look for mini quizzes along the way to learn new and interesting facts!

Look for this symbol, and check your answers on page 64!

Animal Classifications

Exotics
This group of unique creatures is made up of reptiles and amphibians.

Birds
While some birds make good pets, most species, such as macaws and cockatoos, do better in the wild.

Fish
Some fish, such as the betta, are territorial and more aggressive toward other tank mates.

Felines
Cats are born with a natural hunting instinct, and they incorporate this skill into their playing.

Canines

Dogs make loyal companions, but they need to be taken on walks regularly to keep them healthy.

Large Pets

Large pets, such as horses, take a lot of work and are expensive to maintain.

Rodents

This group of small mammals includes hamsters, gerbils, guinea pigs, mice, and rats.

Betta Fish

Did You Know?

Betta fish are not schooling fish and will fight with each other, regardless of gender.

1

2

3

4

5

6

7

Mini Quiz

True or false:
Betta fish are also
known as Siamese
fighting fish.

(Answer on page 64)

9

Bunny

Fun Fact!

Contrary to popular belief, rabbits are not rodents; they are lagomorphs. Rabbits are actually more closely related to horses than they are to rats or mice!

10

Properly socialized rabbits are relatively calm and enjoy being around the people they know.

1

2

3

4

5

6

7

Box Turtle

Pet Details

Size: 5 to 8 inches in length
Location: Asia and North America
Diet: Snails, insects, berries, fungi, slugs, worms, roots, flowers, fish, frogs, salamanders, snakes, birds, and eggs

Fun Fact!

Box turtles can live more than 100 years!

A box turtle is able to draw its head and limbs completely within its shell, thus resembling a box.

Turtle Power!
The high domed shell of the box turtle makes it too large for most predators to consume.

1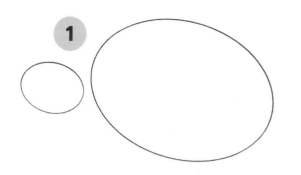

2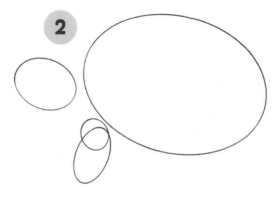

3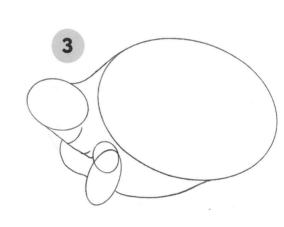

4

5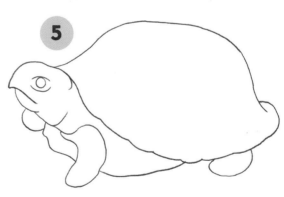

6

7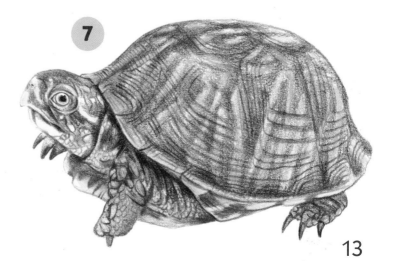

13

Butterfly

The word *Lepidoptera* means "scaly winged" and refers to the microscopic, dust-like scales on butterfly and moth wings.

14

Mini Quiz

How many stages are in the life cycle of a butterfly?

A. 1

B. 2

C. 3

D. 4

(Answer on page 64)

Chinchilla

Pet Details

Size: Up to 14 inches in length, not counting the bushy tail
Weight: Up to 2 pounds
Location: South America, in captivity in the United States
Diet: Plant leaves, fruits, seeds, and small insects, as well as commercial foods made especially for chinchillas

Did You Know?

Chinchillas are native to Chile and Peru, and all that are in captivity in the United States today are descended from the original 13 that were brought into the country in 1927.

These cute little rodents make excellent pets, as they can live up to 20 years and are very social.

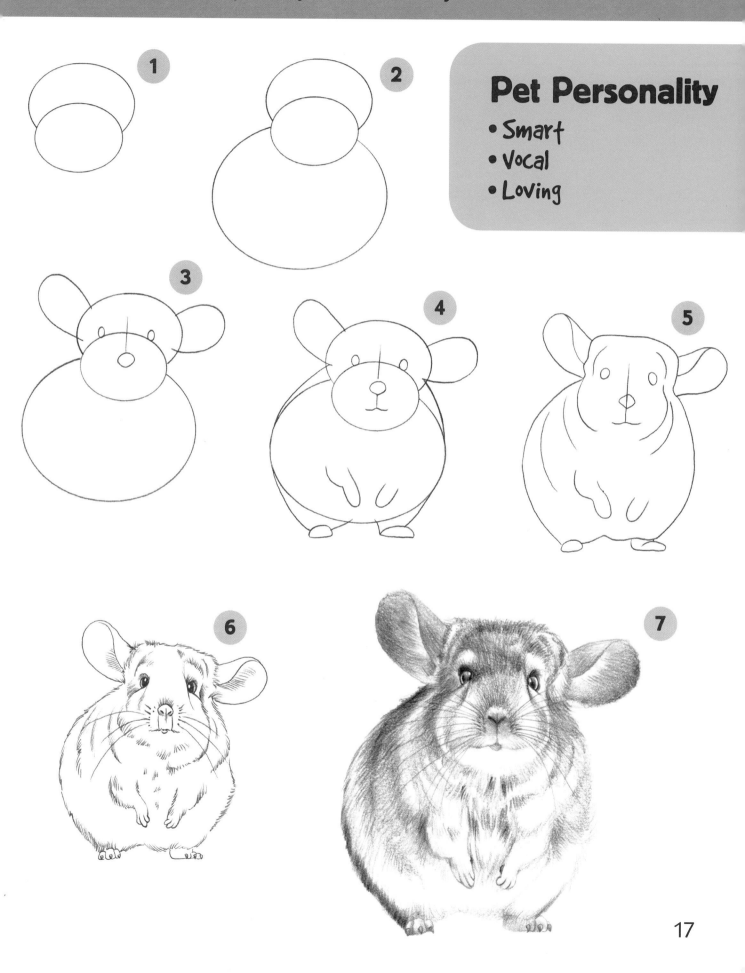

1

2

Pet Personality
- Smart
- Vocal
- Loving

3

4

5

6

7

Chinese Water Dragon

Size: Up to 3 feet in length

Location: East and Southeast Asia

Diet: Insects, small fish, mammals, and reptiles

Fun Fact!

Water dragons have sticky tongues that help them catch and hold their prey!

Water dragons range from dark to light green and have long tails that help them balance.

Mini Quiz

When threatened, water dragons hide in the water. How long can they stay submerged?
A. 5 minutes
B. 15 minutes
C. 25 minutes
D. 60 minutes
(Answer on page 64)

19

Cockatiel

Fun Fact!

Male cockatiels are better at talking and whistling than female cockatiels. In the wild the males use sounds to attract females.

Weight: About 80 to 120 grams

Diet: Grass seeds, berries, nuts, and grains

Size: 10 to 14 inches in length from beak to the tip of the tail

Location: Mainland Australia

Native to Australia, cockatiels are popular throughout the world for their bright, colorful feathers.

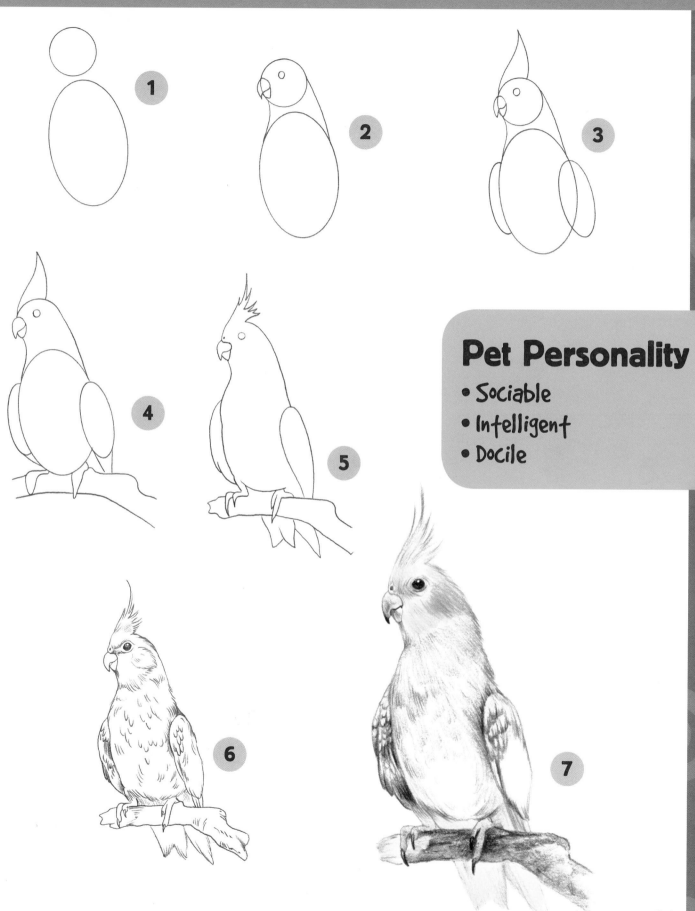

Pet Personality
- Sociable
- Intelligent
- Docile

Ferret

Location: Forests and grasslands

Size: About 20 inches in length

Weight: 2 pounds

Diet: In the wild they hunt mice, small rabbits, and birds

Did You Know?

There are two species of ferret: the common ferret and the black-footed ferret. Domesticated ferrets are common ferrets, but the wild, black-footed ferret is an endangered species.

Ferrets are popular pets, as they become tame, playful, and extremely dependent on their owners when kept in captivity.

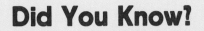
Frog

Did You Know?

Although amphibians can live both on land and in water, frogs must live near swamps, ponds, and in damp places, as they will die if their skin dries out.

Fun Fact!

Frogs use their eyes to help them swallow food! When the frog blinks, its eyeballs are pushed down, creating a bulge in the roof of its mouth, which helps push the food down its throat.

This amphibian can see forward, upward, and sideways all at the same time.

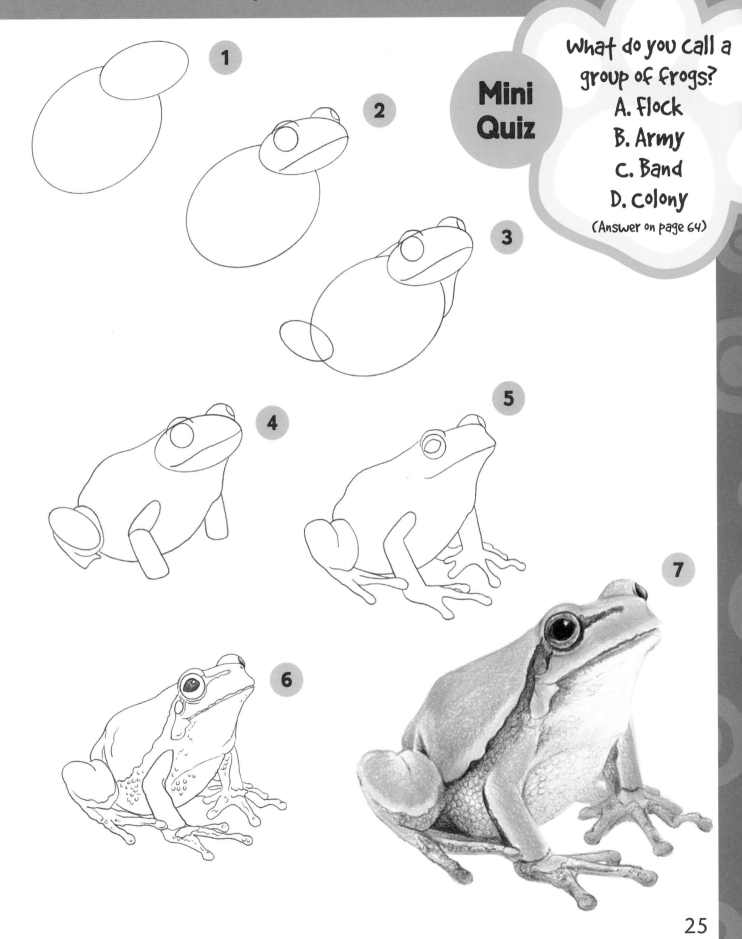

Mini Quiz

What do you call a group of frogs?
A. Flock
B. Army
C. Band
D. Colony
(Answer on page 64)

25

Gecko

Size: 1.2 to 6 inches long, including the tail

Diet: Insects

Location: Warm areas worldwide

Fun Fact!

If detached, a gecko's tail can quickly grow back and be restored to its original shape.

This cute little lizard is found in warm areas throughout the world, with a few species on every continent except Antarctica.

1

2

3

4

5

6

7

Mini Quiz

True or false: Geckos are mostly nocturnal.

(Answer on page 64)

27

Golden Retriever

Fun Fact!

The Golden Retriever is considered by most to be the best breed for service dogs.

Did You Know?

Golden Retrievers were bred in Scotland in the 1800s as water retrievers.

28

Golden Retrievers make excellent family pets due to their gentle, loyal, enthusiastic, and playful nature.

Pet Personality
• Intelligent
• obedient
• Loving

Goldfish

Did You Know?

A popular house pet, the goldfish is omnivorous, feeding on plants and small animals.

The common goldfish has been bred so that it comes in an array of colors, including black, white, yellow, orange, and the golden color for which it is best known.

Mini Quiz

About how many eggs do goldfish lay at mating time?

A. 10

B. 100

C. 1,000

D. 2,000

(Answer on page 64)

Guinea Pig

Size: 8 to 16 inches long

Weight: 1 to 3 pounds

Diet: Vegetables, leafy greens, fruit, and hay

Guinea pigs do not need to drink water if the food they eat is sufficiently moist, but they must have water if fed dry commercial food.

Location: South America

Native to South America, this rodent has a large head and body with small ears and short legs.

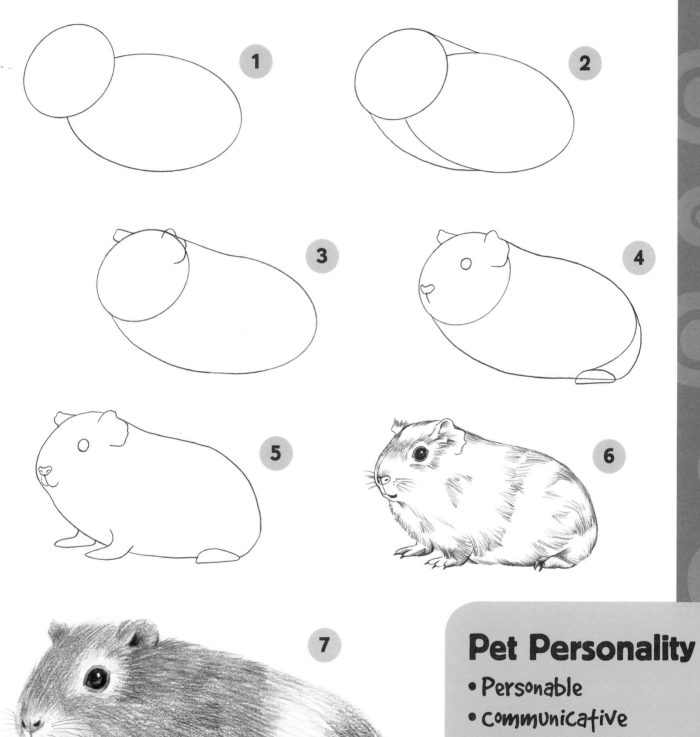

1

2

3

4

5

6

7

Pet Personality
- Personable
- Communicative
- Clean

Jack Russell Terrier

Diet: Food high in protein and grain

Size: 12 to 14 inches tall

Weight: 13 to 17 pounds

Did You Know?

Jack Russell Terriers make great companions as long as they are exercised regularly. They should be taken on long, brisk walks daily and should have some space to run and play.

The Jack Russell Terrier, originally bred in 19th-century England to hunt foxes, is known for its energy, tenacity, and courage.

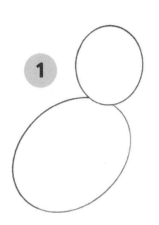

1

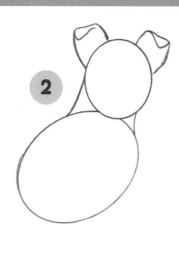

2

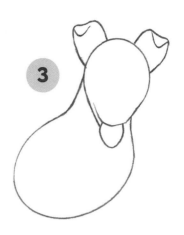

3

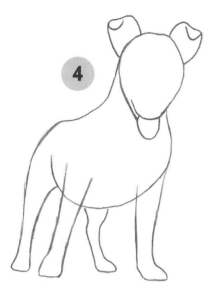

4

5

Pet Personality
- Intelligent
- Loving
- Fearless

6

7

Hamster

Did You Know?

Hamsters have spacious pouches in their cheeks to store food.

Fun Fact!

It is illegal to own a pet hamster in Hawaii! Because the climate is similar to a hamster's natural habitat, officials are afraid that escaped hamsters could establish wild colonies and destroy crops and native plants.

36

The hamster, a burrowing rodent native to western Asia, looks similar to a rat but has a short, robust body with thick, soft fur.

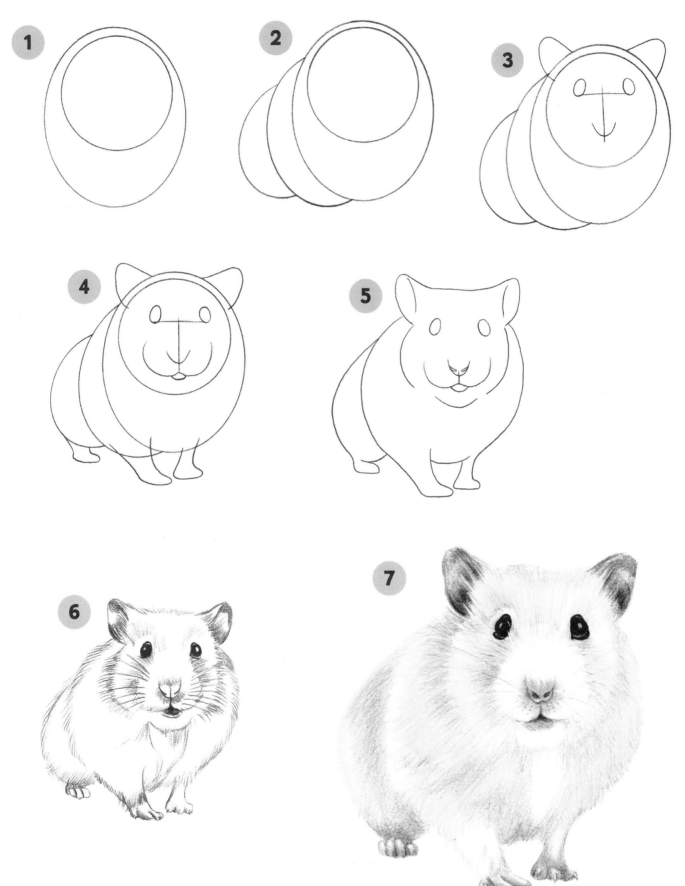

Hedgehog

Pet Details

Size: 5.5 to 12 inches in length
Weight: 1.5 to 2 pounds
Location: Europe, Asia, and Africa
Diet: Insects, snails, slugs, frogs and toads, lizards, snakes, bird eggs, and fruit

Did You Know?

Hedgehogs are solitary creatures, leaving their mothers at only 6 to 13 weeks old to live completely on their own. They like to live alone and are quite territorial.

This insectivore has several thousand short, smooth spines all over its body, as well as excellent hearing and sense of smell.

Fun Fact!

Hedgehogs have a muscle that runs along their neck down to their bottom that allows them to roll up into a protective ball of hard, prickly spines.

Hermit Crab

Did You Know?

All hermit crabs are born in the ocean, even though some species live on land as adults.

Hermit crabs have a soft abdomen with no natural protective shield against predators, so they use empty snail shells for protection and shelter.

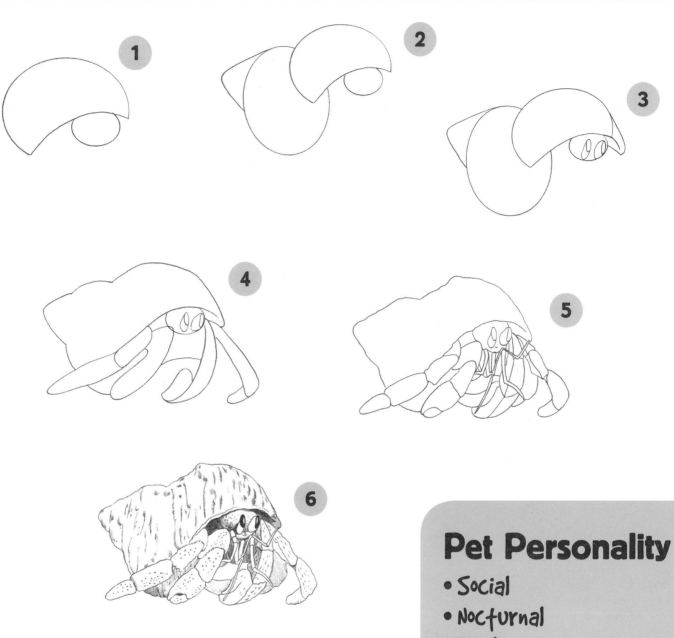

Pet Personality
- Social
- Nocturnal
- Docile

Horse

Fun Fact!

Because their eyes are on the sides of their heads, horses are able to see nearly 360 degrees at one time.

Horses have played a very important role in human civilization, providing transportation and assisting in work.

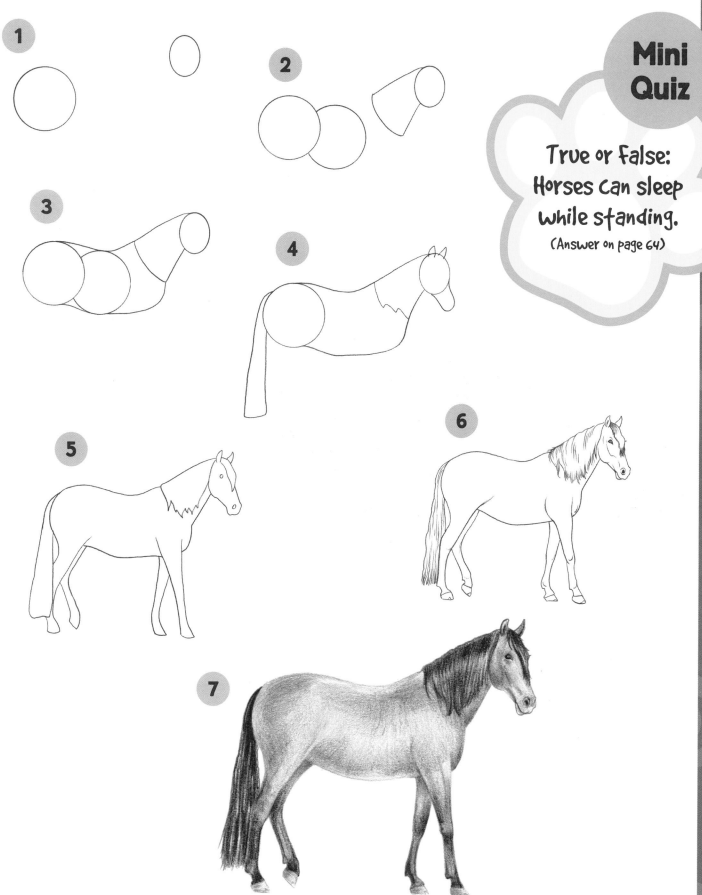

Mini Quiz

True or false: Horses can sleep while standing.

(Answer on page 64)

1

2

3

4

5

6

7

43

Green Iguana

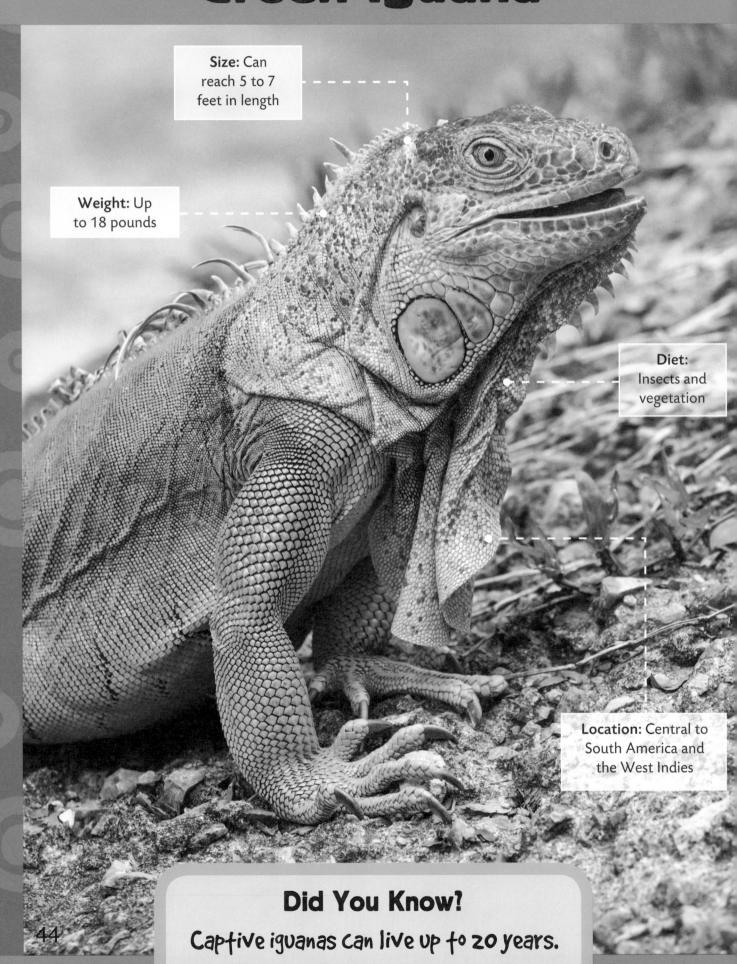

Size: Can reach 5 to 7 feet in length

Weight: Up to 18 pounds

Diet: Insects and vegetation

Location: Central to South America and the West Indies

Did You Know?
Captive iguanas can live up to 20 years.

In the wild, green iguanas are social creatures,
usually found sunbathing and foraging in groups.

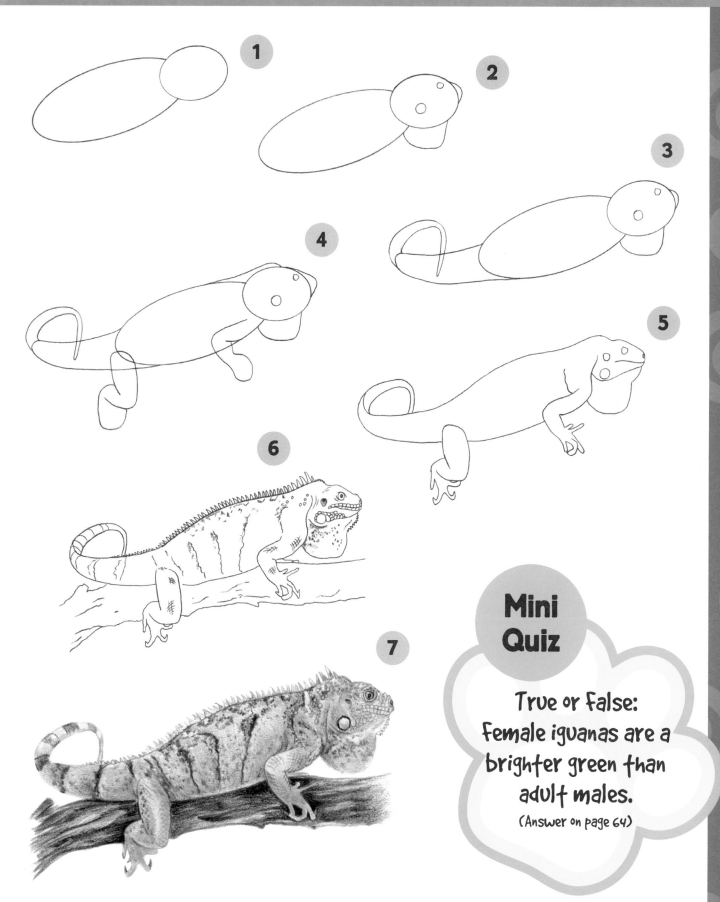

1

2

3

4

5

6

7

Mini Quiz

True or false:
Female iguanas are a
brighter green than
adult males.
(Answer on page 64)

Kitten

Did You Know?

If properly taken care of, cats can live up to 20 years or more!

Fun Fact!

Cats have excellent night vision due to a layer of cells in the eye that reflects light back through the retina, allowing them to see in very low light. This is why cats' eyes glow in the dark!

46

Kittens are cute, curious little balls of energy that love to play.

Pet Personality
- Playful
- Rambunctious
- Loving

47

Lop-eared Rabbit

Did You Know?

The five breeds of lop-eared rabbits are the Mini Lop, the French Lop, the Holland Lop, the American Fuzzy Lop, and the English Lop. Despite its name, the Mini Lop, weighing between 5.5 and 6.5 pounds, is not the smallest breed; the Holland Lop is the smallest, weighing between 2 and 4 pounds.

The five breeds of lop-eared rabbits all have lop ears
but vary in fur length and texture, size, weight, and color.

Mini
Quiz

Which of the following
lop-eared rabbit
breeds is the largest?
A. American Fuzzy Lop
B. French Lop
C. Holland Lop
D. English Lop
(Answer on page 64)

Macaw

Did You Know?

The cobalt-blue Hyacinth Macaw is the largest of all parrots, measuring 37.5 to 39.5 inches long.

Fun Fact!

Male and female macaws look exactly alike, exhibiting the same bright plumage!

Macaws are social and intelligent animals that can be found in Central and South America.

Pet Personality
• Intelligent
• Social
• Easily tamed

Mini Quiz

True or false: Several species of macaws are on the endangered and critically endangered species list.

(Answer on page 64)

Mouse

Pet Details

Size: About 3.5 inches long, not including the tail
Weight: .5 to 1 ounce
Location: Worldwide
Diet: Commercial rodent food and small amounts of fresh fruit and vegetables

Did You Know?

Male and female mice should not be housed together since they breed quickly and produce large litters.

Mice are very social animals, but they are fragile and must be handled gently.

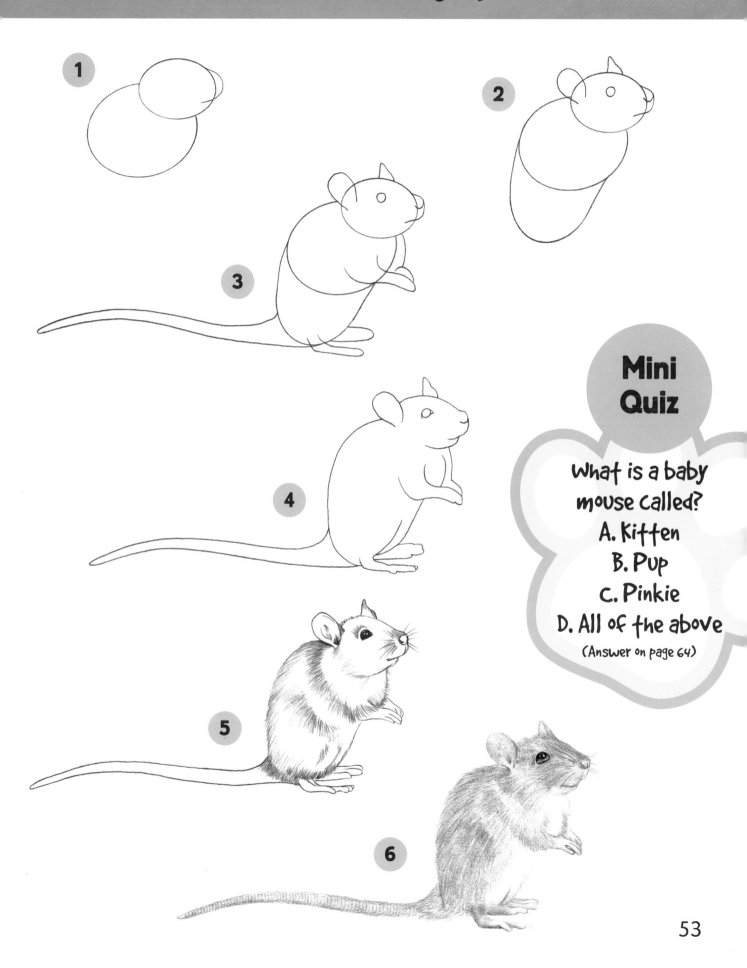

Mini Quiz

What is a baby mouse called?
A. Kitten
B. Pup
C. Pinkie
D. All of the above
(Answer on page 64)

Persian Cat

Fun Fact!

Persians have the longest and thickest fur of all domestic cats. This breed's fur can grow up to 5 inches in length!

Also known as Persian Longhairs, these cats have flat, round faces; small ears; and long, plush fur.

1

2

3

4

5

6

7

Pet Personality
- Loyal
- Gentle
- Loving

Did You Know?
Persians require daily grooming in order to keep their fur from matting.

Potbellied Pig

Fun Fact!

Pigs do not like to be hugged or handled, so no cuddling with this pet!

Did You Know?

Pigs are extremely sensitive to the sun, so they like to roll around in the mud to keep cool and protect their skin.

This unique pet is intelligent and can be easily trained, just like a dog.

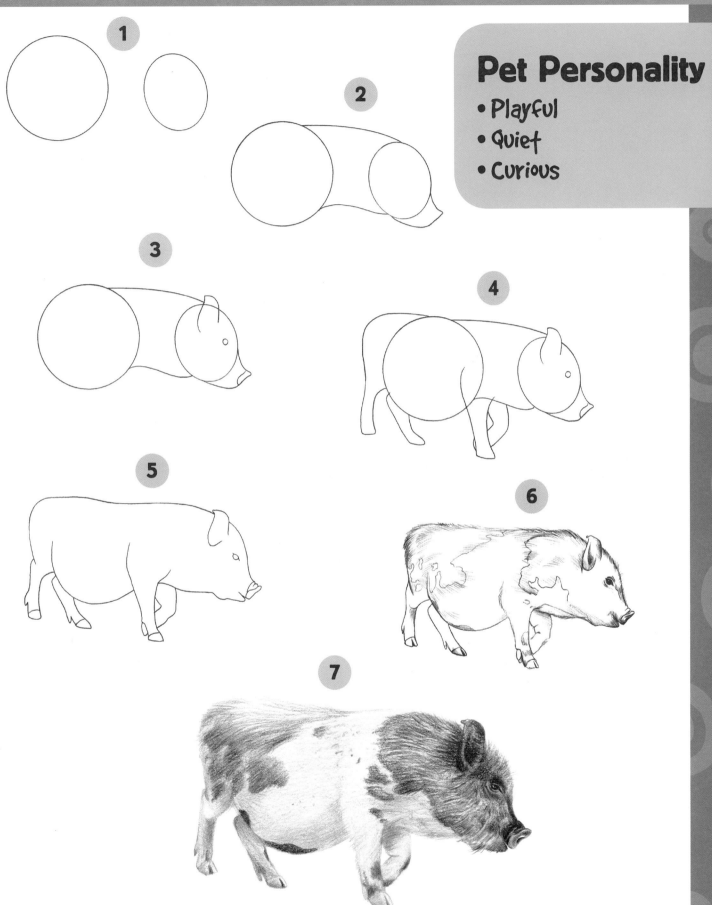

Pet Personality
- Playful
- Quiet
- Curious

Snake

Did You Know?
Snakes can live for more than 20 years, so they require long-term commitment.

Fun Fact!
Snakes are thought to have evolved from lizards in the mid-Cretaceous period, about 100 million years ago!

Snakes cannot bite food; they have flexible jaws
that allow them to swallow their prey whole.

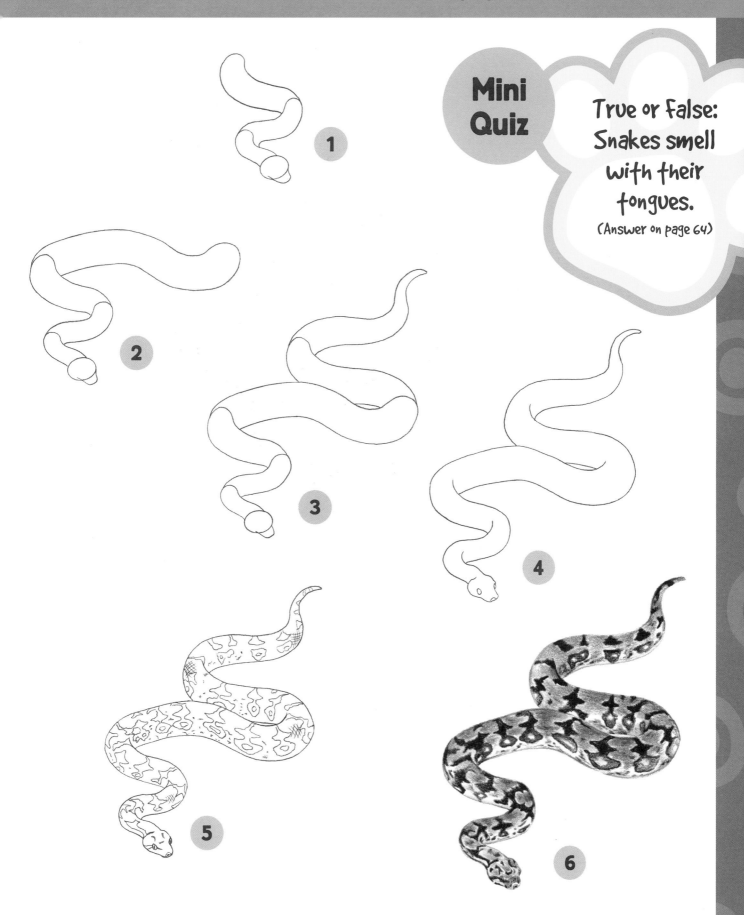

Mini Quiz

True or false:
Snakes smell
with their
tongues.
(Answer on page 64)

Sugar Glider

Size: About 14 inches, including the tail

Weight: About 115 to 140 grams

Diet: Insects, lizards, small birds, nectar, acacia seeds, bird eggs, and native fruits

Location: Forests; native to Australia, Indonesia, and New Guinea

Fun Fact!

Sugar gliders have a flap of loose skin that extends from the fifth finger to the first toe on each side of their bodies, allowing them to literally glide in the air from tree to tree.

This nocturnal marsupial is native to Australia and is also known as a gliding possum.

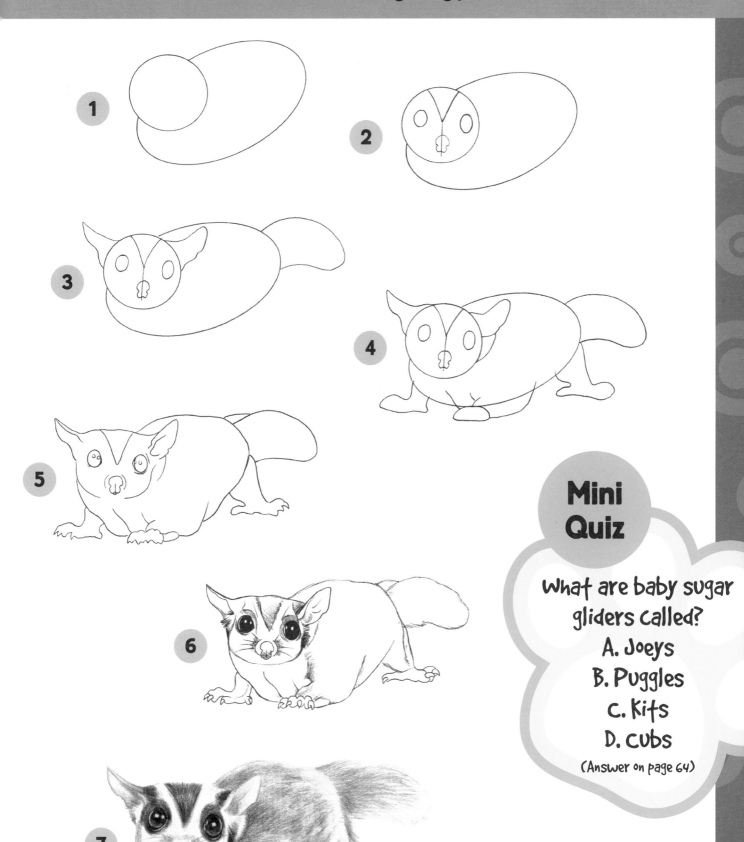

1

2

3

4

5

6

7

Mini Quiz

What are baby sugar gliders called?
A. Joeys
B. Puggles
C. Kits
D. Cubs
(Answer on page 64)

Tarantula

Did You Know?
The hairs on a
tarantula's body are
very sensitive to touch,
temperature, and smell.

These large, hairy spiders live in warm areas,
such as rainforests and deserts, around the world.

Fun Fact!

The largest species of tarantula is found in South America; they have a body length that reaches almost 3 inches! These huge spiders have been known to capture and eat small birds.

Mini Quiz Answers

Page 9: True. Betta fish get this name due to their aggressive nature.

Page 11: True. Training a rabbit to use a litter box is relatively easy because they usually designate a corner of their cage as their "bathroom."

Page 15: D. A butterfly's life cycle has four stages: egg, larva (caterpillar), pupa (chrysalis), and adult (imago).

Page 19: C. Water dragons can stay underwater for as long as 25 minutes.

Page 25: B. A group of frogs is called an "army" of frogs, while a group of toads is called a "knot" of toads.

Page 27: True. There are some species of geckos that only ever come out at night.

Page 31: C. A goldfish lays about 1,000 eggs, the young hatching in three to seven days.

Page 43: True. A horse is able to lock one of its hind legs at the knee, allowing the leg to hold in place until it gets tired; then it will switch and lock the other leg.

Page 45: True. Female and young male iguanas are a much brighter green than adult male iguanas.

Page 49: B. French Lops weigh between 10 and 13 pounds.

Page 51: True. Three macaw species are classified as critically endangered and five are classified as endangered on the IUCN Red List of Threatened Species.

Page 53: D. A baby mouse is referred to as all three of these names.

Page 59: True. Even though snakes have nostrils, they actually flick their tongues in the air, picking up tiny chemical particles, which are then perceived as scent.

Page 61: A. Baby kangaroos, koalas, and wallabies are also known as joeys.